# DISGUSTING & DREADFUL SCIENCE

# Stinky Skunks

## and other animal adaptations

**by Barbara Taylor**

## Crabtree Publishing Company

www.crabtreebooks.com

# Crabtree Publishing Company
www.crabtreebooks.com
1-800-387-7650

**Published in Canada**
**Crabtree Publishing**
616 Welland Avenue
St. Catharines, ON
L2M 5V6

**Published in the United States**
**Crabtree Publishing**
PMB 59051
350 Fifth Ave, 59th Floor
New York, NY 10118

Printed in Hong Kong/082014/BK20140613

**Author:** Barbara Taylor
**Editorial director:** Kathy Middleton
**Editor:** Anastasia Suen
**Proofreader:** Wendy Scavuzzo
**Prepress technician:** Katherine Berti
**Print and production coordinator:** Katherine Berti

Produced by Penny Worms & Graham Rich, Book Packagers

Published by Crabtree Publishing Company in 2015

First published in 2014 by Franklin Watts
(a division of Hachette Children's Books)
Copyright © Franklin Watts 2014

**Picture acknowledgements**:
**Dreamstime:** 15b (Eric Isselee). **George I Matsumoto/Monterey Bay Aquarium Research Institute:** 28b. **iStockphoto.com:** title page (Dean Murray), eyeball cartoon (Elaine Barker), 23b and cover (GlobalP). **Nature Picture Library:** 29t (David Shale), 29b (Solvin Zanki). **Shutterstock.com:** angry monster cartoon (Yayayoyo), cover claws (Christos Georghiou), 4b and cover (DM7), 5tl (Eric Isselee), 5tr (photobar), 5b (Dora Zett), 6t and cover (Michael Rosskothen), 7t (Matt9122), 8 (beltsazar), 9t (fivespots and Sergey Mikhaylov), 9br (Scott E Read), 9bl (Vadim Petrakov), 10t (Butterfly hunter), 10b (LehaKoK), 11t (outdoorsman), 11br (Tory Kallman and Achim Baque), 12tl (Critterbitz), 12b (Beverly Speed and ostill), 13tl (Jamen Percy), 14b (Audrey Snider-Bell), 14t (hxbdzxy), 15tl (Peter Waters), 15m (Eric Isselee), 16t (Juan Gaertner), 16b (Gallinago_media), 17t (pan demin), 17m (Pan Xunbin), 17 louse (Miramiska), 17 flea (Cosmin Manci), 18t (Liusa), 18b (Cathy Keifer), 19m (Silke Baron),19b (Dario Sabljak), 20t (Banzainer), 20b and cover (Angel DiBilio), 21t (Tyler Fox), 21m (John Michael Evan Potter), 21b (Atovot), 22b (Ryan M Bolton), 23t (Matt Jepson), 24b (Dirk Ercken), 24t (John A Andersen), 25t and cover (Aleksey Stemmer), 25b (Rich Carey), 26 (Eric Isselee), 27t (bikeriderlondon), 27bl (anat chant), 27br (Jakkrit Orrasri), 29m (Chiffa). **Twentieth Century Fox Film/ The Kobal Collection:** 13tr. **Wikimedia:** 4t (Olin Feurbacher, US Geological Survey); 6b (Reconstruction by Bashford Dean in 1909), 7b (Dianne Bray/Museum Victoria), 28t (OpenCage).

**All other illustrations by Graham Rich**

Every attempt has been made to clear copyright. Should there be any inadvertent omission, please apply to the publisher for rectification.

**Library and Archives Canada Cataloguing in Publication**

Taylor, Barbara, 1954-, author
     Stinky skunks and other animal adaptations / Barbara Taylor.

(Disgusting & dreadful science)
Includes index.
Issued in print and electronic formats.
ISBN 978-0-7787-1420-0 (bound).--ISBN 978-0-7787-1424-8 (pbk.).--
ISBN 978-1-4271-9358-2 (pdf).--ISBN 978-1-4271-9354-4 (html)

          1. Animal defenses--Juvenile literature.  2. Animals--Adaptation--
Juvenile literature.  I. Title.

QL759.T39 2014          j591.47          C2014-903953-0
                                          C2014-903954-9

**Library of Congress Cataloging-in-Publication Data**

Taylor, Barbara, 1954- author.
Stinky skunks and other animal adaptations / by Barbara Taylor.
     pages cm. -- (Disgusting & dreadful science)
Includes index.
 ISBN 978-0-7787-1420-0 (reinforced library binding) -- ISBN 978-0-7787-1424-8 (pbk.) --
ISBN 978-1-4271-9358-2 (electronic pdf) -- ISBN 978-1-4271-9354-4 (electronic html)
1.  Adaptation (Biology)--Juvenile literature. 2.  Animal behavior--Juvenile literature.
I. Title.

QH546.T39 2015
591.4--dc23

                    2014022794

# Contents

# Survive or die

It's a hairy, scary, dog-eat-dog world out there and animals are constantly fighting to survive. Only those best adapted live to fight another day. Adaptations **include what** an animal looks like, how its body works, how it behaves, and the way it uses its surroundings to keep itself alive. They include disgusting feeding methods, dreadful defense strategies, and cunning ways to beat the challenges of living in extreme environments.

Ouch!

Life survives on Earth in the most unlikely places. The rare Devil's Hole pupfish survives in hot springs in North America in water so hot that other fish would cook in it!

AAGGHHH!!!

AAGGHHH!!!

## KING lizards

Dinosaurs were probably the most successful animals that have ever lived. They ruled the world for over 150 million years and developed into at least 1,000 different kinds, from terrifying tyrannosaurs to peaceful plant-eaters. Dinosaurs died out about 65 million years ago, possibly due to huge volcanic eruptions, climate change, or a giant **comet** hitting Earth. Some dinosaurs had feathers and many scientists believe that they did not die out completely, but some developed into birds. So the relatives of feathered dinosaurs may be super survivors, still living with us today!

# Spot the difference

Animals living in different parts of the world sometimes look similar because they have adapted to the same environment. The green tree python of New Guinea looks like the emerald tree boa of South America, yet these snakes live thousands of miles (kilometers) apart. They both live in rain forest trees and are well **camouflaged** among the green leaves. Both snakes also coil around tree branches and reach out to catch birds as they fly past.

EASY...

**Emerald tree boa**

**Green tree python**

## See for Yourself

### Doggy discoveries

It is hard to believe that people have developed more than 100 breeds of dog from the huge variety of **characteristics** hidden inside just one wild dog – the wolf. When you are out for a walk, see how many different kinds of dog you can spot in the street or the park.

## Survival of the fittest

Over time, animals adapt to their surroundings. Those animals with the best adaptations survive to pass on their characteristics to the next generation, while other animals die out. This idea is called the "survival of the fittest," or **natural selection**. It was this idea that led scientists Charles Darwin and Alfred Russel Wallace to develop the theory of **evolution** in the 19th century.

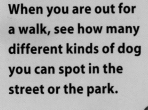

# shark attack!

D o sharks deserve their fearsome reputation? If you're a small sea creature, you bet they do! The things that make sharks seem scary to us, such as their sharp teeth or surprise attacks, are the same things that have helped them to survive on our planet for millions of years. Sharks are perfectly designed underwater hunters. They have been lurking in the oceans since before the time of the dinosaurs.

## Great white

Only a few sharks attack people – and the great white shark is one of them. It's big, heavy, and always hungry. A great white's largest teeth grow as long as a person's finger and have sharp, jagged edges for slicing through flesh. Its jaws can stretch wide enough to swallow a seal whole!

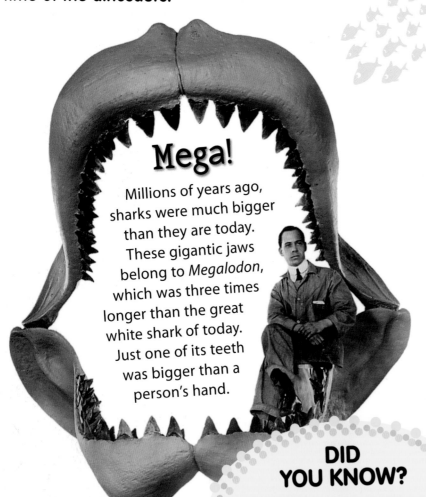

## Mega!

Millions of years ago, sharks were much bigger than they are today. These gigantic jaws belong to *Megalodon*, which was three times longer than the great white shark of today. Just one of its teeth was bigger than a person's hand.

## Ouch!

The cookiecutter shark swivels its sharp ring of teeth in a circle, leaving round, cookie-shaped holes in its victims.

### DID YOU KNOW?

As a shark's teeth wear away or fall out, new teeth take their place, so they never need to go to the dentist!

# See for Yourself

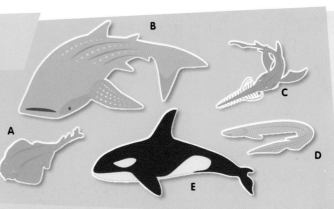

## Odd one out

One of these creatures is not a shark.
Can you spot it?

**Answer:** E is a killer whale (a mammal). The rest are sharks (fish). A is an angel shark, B a whale shark, C a saw shark, D a frilled shark.

## Funny face

A hammerhead shark's eyes and nostrils are far apart, one on each side of its hammer-shaped head. This helps the hammerhead track down its **prey** better than most other sharks. Its favorite prey is stingrays. A hammerhead uses its huge head to pin a stingray to the seabed while it eats its meal. It even eats the stingray's poisonous barb!

# Jaw-dropping!

The long, pointy nose of the goblin shark looks rather like a unicorn's horn. This huge snout is packed with electrical sensors, which help the goblin shark to find prey in the darkness of the deep sea. But the truly amazing thing about goblin sharks is that they have springy jaws that can catapult right out of their mouths to grab prey.

# Monster killers

You might think that monsters belong in films or nightmares, but some real animals do reach unbelievably monstrous sizes! Snakes can be as long as a bus, and bears can weigh as much as a small car. Large animals are strong and powerful enough to attack large prey, and they are unlikely to be attacked themselves. They do, however, need to eat a lot of energy-giving food to provide enough fuel for their big bodies.

## Yuck!

A Komodo dragon (below) has saliva (spit) that contains a deadly cocktail of **bacteria**. Once an animal is bitten by a dragon, it slowly dies of an infection. Several dragons then gather to share the feast.

## Dreadful dragon

This brute of lizard has a terrible temper! It's a Komodo dragon, the world's largest lizard, and it can grow up to 10 feet (3 meters) long. Komodo dragons have even been known to kill and eat people! Usually they hide in bushes or long grass on the island of Komodo in Indonesia, pouncing on deer, wild pigs, and water buffalo in surprise attacks. They can eat up to 80 percent of their body weight in one meal!

# Super spider

The Goliath tarantula is a whopper! It barely fits on a dinner plate. It climbs trees in the forests of South America to attack birds and chicks in their nests. This monster spider is strong enough to kill prey of its own size, although its **venom** is not as strong as that of some smaller spiders.

Shoooo!

# Grrrr-izzly bear

The largest meat-eating **mammal** ever to walk the Earth was the giant short-faced bear. It hunted bison and horses millions of years ago in North America. Today the grizzly bear is king at less than half that size, but it still packs a punch. Grizzlies can crush the skull of a large deer with one swipe of their massive paws.

Bears look even scarier when they stand up on two legs!

# Heavyweight

It takes four people to lift this heavy anaconda, which can weigh as much as three adults! Anacondas live in the rivers of the Amazon rain forest where there is plenty of food, and the water supports their massive weight. Anacondas catch animals as big as deer, caimans, and even jaguars, coiling tightly around their prey until it stops breathing. They then swallow the animal whole.

# Pack power

When animal hunters work together as a team, they become much more powerful and effective at killing their prey. Pack power definitely rules when predators work together to track down prey much larger than themselves. Communication is the key to group success, including chemical signals, sound signals, and body language. Each member of the team has to understand its own job, look after the others, and be prepared to share the spoils of the hunt.

The sting of a fire ant causes a burning sensation on the skin. This poor insect doesn't stand a chance!

## Angry ants

These red ants are also called fire ants because they have a painful sting. They are very aggressive, and together they can attack and overcome larger insects and other small prey.

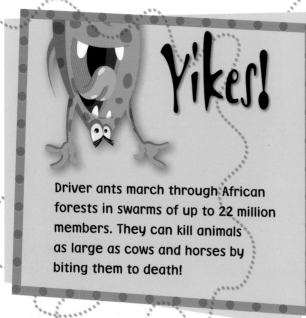

## Yikes!

Driver ants march through African forests in swarms of up to 22 million members. They can kill animals as large as cows and horses by biting them to death!

## Feeding frenzy

South American piranhas have a fearsome reputation, but only four species are dangerous. The red-bellied piranha, (above) look innocent, but they use their razor-sharp teeth to quickly strip the flesh from prey such as larger fish and birds. The water looks as if it's boiling as they all try to feed at the same time.

# Company of wolves

Intelligent and adaptable animals, wolves live in packs of between 8 and 20 family members. By working together, a pack of wolves can overcome and kill animals as large as musk oxen or moose, but they usually hunt sick, old, and injured animals. Wolves have excellent senses and their eerie howls help them to keep in touch with each other. When they howl together, it can sound super scary!

# Killer whales

Behind you!

Orcas (killer whales) live in family groups, called pods. These cunning hunters plan their attacks. They sometimes swim together to create a large wave that tips seals off floating slabs of ice and into their waiting jaws!

 ## See for Yourself

### Make an ant farm

You will need a 2-liter plastic bottle and a 1-liter plastic bottle, a funnel, tape, black paper, white paper, scissors, soil or sand, ants (not fire ants!)

1. Cut the tops off both bottles and put the small bottle inside the large one. Use the funnel to fill the space between the two bottles with soil.

2. Ask an adult to help you collect the ants (be careful—some ants sting!) and add them to the soil.

3. Tape a circle of white paper over the top of the large bottle and make tiny holes in it so the ants can breathe, but can't escape! Cover the outside with black paper.

4. Remove the paper when you want to watch the ants and see their tunnels.

5. Return the ants to the outdoors after a few days.

# Lethal weapons

Bald eagles grab and kill prey by piercing its flesh with their powerful talons (claws).

**C**an you imagine having sharp knives on your fingers, or teeth as long as your arm? Well, animals such as eagles and wolverines use their knife-like claws to catch their prey and a hippo's teeth grow up to 20 inches (51 cm) long! Many animals are armed and dangerous in this way – showing just how weak and feeble humans really are.

## DID YOU KNOW?

Secretary birds stomp or kick snakes to death and swallow them whole.

Mantis shrimp

POW...

## Pack a punch

Mantis shrimp punch crabs, clams, and snails with their club-like legs, smashing through their shells with a force as deadly as a bullet. These super shrimp pack the most powerful punch of any animal.

# Crampon claws

Wolverines use their claws like climber's **crampons** to help them climb steep cliffs in the mountains of North America. These fearless predators attack prey as large as moose by sinking their powerful claws into the animal's back and holding on until the animal collapses. Their teeth are strong enough to crunch through bones, fresh or frozen!

The superhero Wolverine, part of the X-men team, has claws that shoot out from the backs of his hands.

Wolverine

Moose

# Open wide

Did you know that hippos are one of the most dangerous animals in Africa? Their huge tusks can make holes in the side of a wooden boat, and they can kill people or crocodiles if they feel threatened. But they usually only use their impressive tusks for self-defense, or for fighting rivals.

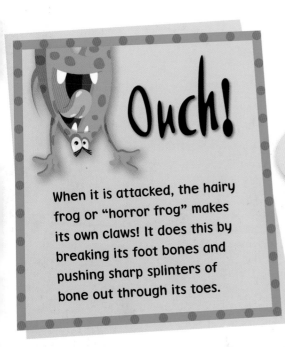

## Ouch!

When it is attacked, the hairy frog or "horror frog" makes its own claws! It does this by breaking its foot bones and pushing sharp splinters of bone out through its toes.

Male hippos yawn widely, but they aren't tired. They are saying...

*Look how big my tusks are!*

13

# Animal cannibals

**A**nimal cannibals **eat animals of their own kind. But why do they have such disgusting feeding habits? Well, sometimes, there is just not enough food to go around, so it's a matter of survival…** Female animals may also eat their mates, or even their own young, to give them the extra strength they need to reproduce. Some male animals kill babies that are not their own to give their own young a better chance of survival.

## Beware crocodiles!

A crocodile will snap up anything that wanders too close to its sharp teeth – even its own young! Baby crocodiles are too small to defend themselves, so they make bite-sized meals for the adults.

**Only two percent of hatchlings survive to grow into adults.**

# Eating for energy

Most snakes lay eggs, but a female rattlesnake's eggs hatch inside her body. This means that she gives birth to baby snakes. Some of these babies are not alive when they are born and many mother rattlesnakes eat their dead babies. This helps them to replace some of the energy they use up during pregnancy and birth.

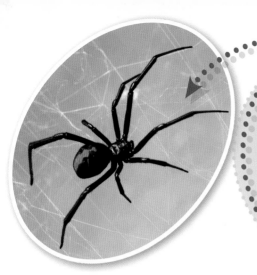

Female black widow spiders will eat more or less anything moving on their web. So males have to tread very carefully! They shake the web in a way that says: "I'm here to mate, don't eat me!"

# Yuck!

Baby tiger sharks are cannibals even before they are born! About 16–23 eggs start to develop inside the mother, but only two baby sharks are born. That's because they've eaten their siblings so they can grow big and strong.

How old are you, kid?

Six months today... honest!

# Male pride

When a male lion takes over a new group, or pride, of lions, he kills all the cubs under six months old. Then he mates with the lionesses, who will give birth to his own cubs.

# Sibling snacks

Young fire salamander **larvae** such as this one may look tiny and helpless, but they have a big appetite! Hungry larvae grab anything moving that looks or feels like food, even their own brothers and sisters. Tiger salamanders have two kinds of larvae – a small one that feeds on water creatures and a larger cannibal version that eats the smaller one. That's one sure-fire way of wiping out the competition!

# Eating us

Welcome to the creepy world of some of the disgusting and dreadful creatures that feed on us. They can cause harm, disease, or even death. These uninvited guests, called parasites, don't usually want to kill us – that would be silly because their food supply would be cut off! Instead, they want an easy life, clinging on tightly and feeding on ready-made meals.

## Gutsy worm

The tapeworm is a delightful worm that sometimes finds a nice home inside a person's guts (intestines), stealing food as it moves past. The hooks on the top of a tapeworm's head keep it firmly attached to the gut wall. Tapeworms can survive like this for years…

## Monster mosquito

The female mosquito is the most dangerous insect in the world. She feeds on human blood because she needs the **proteins** for her eggs to develop. When female mosquitoes suck human blood, they may pass parasites into our bodies, including the parasites that cause **malaria**. Mosquito bites cause the deaths of more than one million people every year.

### Yuck!

Tapeworms usually grow about 10-16 feet (3-5 meters) long but the longest ones reach lengths of over 66 feet (20 meters)!

**3** *Full up!*

**1** *Hungry...*

**2** *Feeding...*

The itchy bumps around mosquito bites are caused by the way your body reacts to the mosquito's saliva.

16

# Blood suckers

Leeches feed on blood. For hundreds of years, leeches were used by doctors who thought they removed "bad blood" from patients and kept their bodies working properly. Leeches produce special chemicals that keep the blood flowing until they are full. In just one meal, a leech may grow up to ten times its normal size! Leeches are still used by some modern doctors to control blood flow following surgery.

Adult blood flukes are only less than an inch (1–2 cm) long! They are most common in tropical countries.

## Blood fluke

The blood fluke is a nasty parasitic worm that spends part of its life in freshwater snails and the other part in any person who wades, bathes or swims in water full of infected snails. Blood flukes go through a person's skin and set up home inside their veins. They can make a person very sick, damaging **organs**, such as the liver and lungs.

# See for Yourself
## Parasite differences

**Head lice and fleas are parasites, too. Do you know the difference? Here's a quick guide.**

1. It jumps.  Flea   It scuttles.  Louse   A

2. Long back legs.  Flea   Short legs with claws.  Louse   B

3. Red-brown and flat.  Flea   Dark gray and oval.  Louse

4. It bites.  Flea   It makes you itchy.  Louse

5. On your pet.  Flea   In someone's hair.  Louse

**Now look at the pictures. Which is which?**

A is the louse. B is the flea.

# Creepy camouflage

**N**ow you see me, now you don't! Both predators and prey are experts at playing hide-and-seek. Colors and patterns that help animals to blend in with their surroundings are called camouflage. Camouflaged predators get really close to their prey before making a surprise attack. Camouflaged prey are hard to see when they keep very still. Some animals can even change color. Babies need extra protection so they are often better camouflaged than their parents.

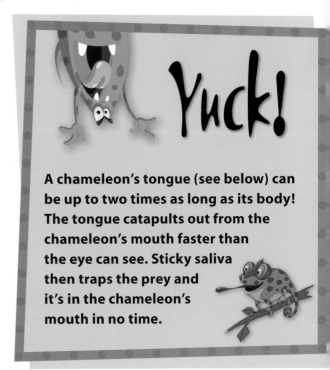

## Yuck!

A chameleon's tongue (see below) can be up to two times as long as its body! The tongue catapults out from the chameleon's mouth faster than the eye can see. Sticky saliva then traps the prey and it's in the chameleon's mouth in no time.

## Crafty chameleon

Many people think that chameleons are the masters of camouflage, but not all chameleons can change color to match their background. If they can, it allows them to get very close to tasty insects, which they trap on the end of their long, sticky tongue. However, most chameleons change color when they are fighting or frightened, or when the day gets brighter and hotter and the evening becomes darker and cooler. Patches of color in their skin move around or become bigger or smaller to change their appearance.

ZAP!

## See for Yourself

### Hide-and-seek

Try wearing green or brown clothes and playing hide-and-seek in the park or garden. Use face paints to help you blend in with the background. Stripes, spots, or blotches of color will break up the shape of your face and make you harder to see.

# Master of disguise

The painted frogfish doesn't look much like a fish. It looks more like a piece of **coral** or rock. Small fish swim right up to the frogfish without realizing the danger they are in. Then, suddenly, the frogfish opens its mouth very wide and gulps them down – just like a frog.

# Spot the octopus

Octopuses hide right in front of your very eyes by changing color to blend in with the background. They use colors and muscles in their skin to match the colors, patterns, and textures of their surroundings. Sharks and other predators just swim right on by. Unwary prey, such as crabs and shellfish, are easy meals.

Octopuses also have colorful mood swings. They turn white when they are afraid, and red when they are angry!

# Poop and pee

**N**othing in nature is wasted – not even poop and pee! A few animals go as far as eating their own poop, and one animal's poop may become a tasty lunch for another animal. But some animals prefer to wear a poopy disguise. It's a good way of saying "Don't eat this!" Pee is just as useful. Animals spray pee around their home area to tell other animals "I live here! keep out!" It's also great stuff for keeping cool (don't try this at home).

## Hikers beware!

If you are hiking in the Rocky Mountains in North America, it's best to pee well away from trails. Why? Because mountain goats like to lick human pee for the salt it contains. And they have very sharp horns!

*It feels good!*

## Cool dude

When we sweat, moisture **evaporates** from our skin into the air, taking heat away from our bodies and cooling us down. Turkey vultures don't sweat. Instead, they pee on their legs! As the pee evaporates, it cools them down. This gross habit has an added bonus. The pee helps to kill any bacteria, keeping the vultures clean and healthy.

# Yuck!

When hippos poop in their river homes, they spin their tails like a propeller to create a "dung shower" that covers the widest possible area. Predators and rivals keep well away!

## What *is* that?

Some swallowtail caterpillars look like bird droppings on green leaves. Birds ignore these caterpillars because they don't recognize them as a possible snack. When the caterpillars grow too big to look like bird droppings, they turn bright green, making them hard to see among the leaves.

## Dung delights

Dung beetles like nothing better than a perfectly rolled ball of fresh poop. The female lays her eggs inside so, when the young hatch out, they have lots of their favorite food to eat. Sweet!

## Bunny poop

Rabbits are poop-eaters, too! They have two types of poop – the dry, round pellets that you see in fields, and a dark, mushy, slimy, smelly type of poop that you don't see because they eat it, sometimes straight from their bottoms! It looks like a small bunch of grapes, and is packed with good bacteria and essential **nutrients**. They eat the dry pellets sometimes, too!

21

# Stinky and squirty

**H**old your nose and stand well back! These animals use all sorts of smelly surprises and shape-shifting tricks to make sure they survive. Stinky sprays don't just smell foul, they can irritate, burn, and even be poisonous. These sprays come out of the rear end, the skin, or even the mouth. A few animals squirt out blood, chop off their tails, or spew out their own guts. That's sacrifice!

**BOOM!**

## Exploding cucumbers!

Some sea cucumbers are able to explode their insides out of their body! They may do this for defense, or as a way of getting rid of nasty waste. Fortunately, the organs regrow – sometimes this takes only a week.

### DID YOU KNOW?

Spitting cobras spray venom into a predator's eyes from as far away as 6.6 feet (2 meters).

## Stinkpot turtle

Stinkpot turtles are named after the foul, musky smell they give off when they feel threatened. These tiny turtles are only about 4 inches (10 cm) long so they are very vulnerable to predators. The terrible smell comes from **glands** along the edge of their shell.

# Tail trick

Many lizards snap off their own tail to escape a predator. The tail wriggles and twitches for a while, distracting the predator long enough for the lizard to run away. The lizard grows a new tail in a few weeks, although this takes a lot of energy.

Weak joints between a lizard's tail bones make the tail easier to break.

# Mega stink

Skunks produce the smelliest liquid in the world to deter predators. You really don't want to get anywhere near a skunk because their smelly spray can cause temporary blindness and injure your nose. The smell also seems to take forever to get rid of! So heed the warning of the skunk's black and white colors and keep well away from this stinky animal.

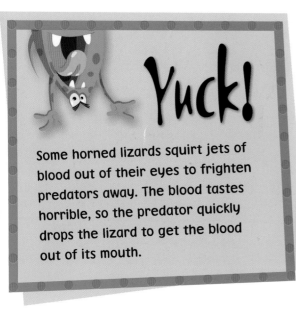

## Yuck!

Some horned lizards squirt jets of blood out of their eyes to frighten predators away. The blood tastes horrible, so the predator quickly drops the lizard to get the blood out of its mouth.

It wasn't me!

# Powerful poisons

Beware of brightly colored animals! Their colors often carry a warning message: "I taste nasty and will make you feel very sick. I might even kill you!" Predators soon learn to heed these warning colors. Some animals make the poisons in their own bodies. Others take in poisons with their food. Poisons may be produced in an animal's skin or stored inside its body and injected through fangs, claws, or stinger.

## Sea bandit

This banded sea snake is ten times more venomous than a rattlesnake! Sea snake venom has to act quickly to stop prey, such as fish, from swimming away. But despite their lethal venom, sea snakes are timid creatures and are not likely to bite people unless threatened.

I'm not just a pretty face...

### Red for danger

It's hard to believe a tiny frog the size of a thumbnail can be deadly dangerous! Yet poison dart frogs have a lethal poison in their skin. They get their poison from the insects they eat.

There may be as many as 45 different toxins in scorpion venom!

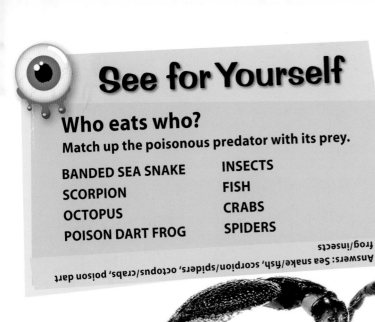

# Sting in the tail

Love them or loathe them, you have to admire scorpions! With sharp stingers and giant claws, they look fearsome, but scorpions are one of life's success stories. They have survived on Earth for hundreds of millions of years. And only about 20 of the 2,000 different kinds are dangerous to humans. Mostly they use their venom to kill or **paralyze** their prey, such as spiders, or to defend themselves. Why? Because making new venom is exhausting!

# Yuck!

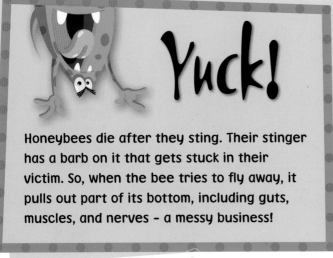

Honeybees die after they sting. Their stinger has a barb on it that gets stuck in their victim. So, when the bee tries to fly away, it pulls out part of its bottom, including guts, muscles, and nerves - a messy business!

# R-eel nasty

Moray eels not only look nasty, but most of them may be coated in a poisonous slime and have poisons in their blood. They produce the stuff themselves, unlike many other poisonous sea creatures, such as pufferfish, who get their poisons from bacteria in the **algae** they eat.

25

# Nighttime terrors

**F**illed with howls, hoots, screeches, and other mysterious sounds, the ghostly blackness of the night seems scary to us. But around half of all land animals come out at night; they are called nocturnal animals. Many prey animals find it easier to hide in the darkness and, in hot, dry places it is easier to keep cool once the sun sets. Super senses, such as keen hearing or eyesight, help nocturnal animals in the fight to survive.

## Black as the night

Leopards and jaguars are usually a golden color with black spots, but sometimes they are dark brown with black spots. This dark coloring helps these smart predators to hide in the jungle and to hunt at night. They glide silently through the trees, using their black invisibility cloak to disappear into the darkness.

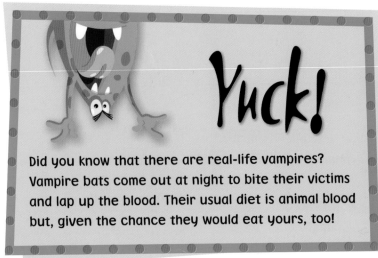

## Yuck!

Did you know that there are real-life vampires? Vampire bats come out at night to bite their victims and lap up the blood. Their usual diet is animal blood but, given the chance they would eat yours, too!

# Night owls

Owls have big eyes and huge **pupils** to let in as much light as possible. Most owls, such as this barn owl, can see in the dark two or three times better than a person. Owls also have excellent hearing, which helps them to attack their prey in the dark. They fly silently, so they can hear their prey then swoop down for a surprise attack.

HELP!

# Bat attack

Claws packed with venom!

Giant centipedes hang from the roof of bat caves and seize bats out of the air as they fly past. Their sharp front claws are loaded with a powerful venom to kill the bats quickly. These huge centipedes can grow to 12 inches (30 cm) long. Their bodies dry out easily, so they come out at night, when the air is cool and damp.

Cockroaches have been scuttling around in the dark since before the time of the dinosaurs. They look the same now as they did then.

Adapt? I'm perfect as I am!

 # See for Yourself

## Attracting night animals

Night animals are hard to spot, but some are attracted to artificial light. Here are ways to attract some to your home to study them.

1. Put a light by a closed window on a summer night. Several different kinds of moths will be attracted by the light and you can watch them from inside.

2. Moths love to eat sweet food. Ask an adult to mash a ripe banana with a tablespoon of beer and some sugar. Paint the sticky mixture onto a fence or tree trunk on a warm summer evening and watch the insects that fly in to feed.

3. Ask an adult to help you set up a camping lantern in front of a white sheet hanging over a gate, fence, or hedge. Which nighttime animals are attracted to your light?

# Deep-sea horrors

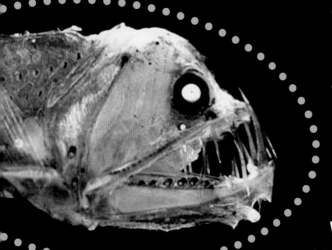

In the freezing cold, inky black waters of the deep sea, the huge weight of water pressing down is so massive that a human diver would be crushed to death in an instant. Deep-sea animals have flabby, watery bodies, which resist being squashed. Food is scarce in the deep sea, but many fish attract their prey with glowing lights. Wickedly sharp teeth and huge stomachs ensure that prey does not escape.

## Toothy trap

Imagine having teeth so long they won't fit inside your mouth. That's what a viperfish (above) has to deal with, but they make an amazing line of daggers for trapping prey! This deep-sea fish can also open its jaws very wide to swallow as much food as possible at each meal. The spots along its side produce glowing lights, which the fish can switch on and off. The flashing lights help to attract prey, confuse enemies, or perhaps send signals to other viperfish.

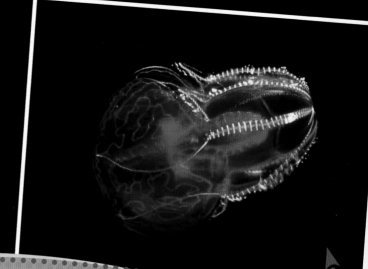

## Can't see me!

The red color of the bloodybelly comb jelly makes it disappear. That's because, in the deep sea, red animals appear black and blend into their dark surroundings. This protects them from predators.

**Here, little fishes.**

# Dragon light

Dragonfish wave the weird, glowing whisker under their chin to attract small fish in the darkness of the deep sea. Some even have "spotlights" beneath their eyes to light up their prey. When a fish swims close by, it is quickly snapped up in the dragon's powerful jaws. It may look gruesome, but if you met a dragonfish, you wouldn't be scared. It's only 6 inches (15 cm) long!

## DID YOU KNOW?

The female anglerfish has a built-in fishing rod growing out of her back! What's more, the tip of the rod glows in the dark to attract prey, such as shrimp and small fish.

# Invisible fish

Hatchetfish have huge eyes to catch as much light as possible. This helps them to navigate and find their prey. The body of a hatchetfish is very thin, which makes it hard for predators to see them head-on.

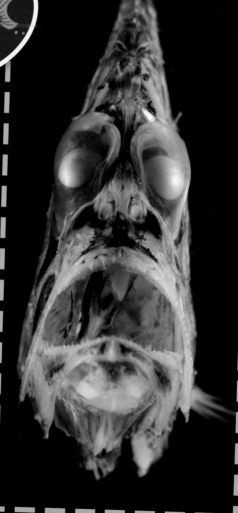

## Yuck!

The gulper eel can swallow prey as large as itself! Its mouth is huge and its stomach stretches to hold these mega-meals.

# Glossary

**adaptations** the ways in which an animal becomes suited to its particular way of life

**algae** microscopic, plant-like living things that usually make their own food.

**bacteria** microscopic, one-celled living things

**camouflaged** has colors, patterns, or shapes that allow it to blend in with its surroundings

**cannibal** an animal that eats animals of the same species

**characteristics** the things that make something distinctive, such as what it looks like

**comet** a ball of rock and ice traveling through space, often seen with a tail of gas and dust

**coral** tiny sea animals whose stony skeletons form coral reefs

**crampons** spikes fixed to a climber's boot

**evaporates** when a liquid changes into a gas as it warms up

**evolution** the gradual change in a species over many generations

**glands** parts of the body that produce substances, such as venom or the liquids skunks and turtles use for defense

**larvae** the immature stage in the life cycle of certain animals, such as insects and frogs

**malaria** a disease caused by a microscopic parasite and spread by mosquitoes

**mammal** an intelligent, hairy, and adaptable animal that feeds its young on mother's milk

**natural selection** the idea that those creatures best adapted to their environment survive and pass on their useful adaptations to their offspring

**nocturnal** active during the night and rests by day

**nutrients** substances that help animals grow and stay healthy

**organ** body parts such as the brain or heart, that have special function

**paralyze** to cause a living thing to become unable to move

**parasites** living things that live on or inside the body of another

**predator** an animal that kills and eats other animals

**proteins** substances in the body that are vital for health, growth, and movement

**prey** an animal that is killed and eaten by a predator

**pupils** the holes through which light enters the eyes

**venom** the poison in the bite or sting of some animals

# Websites and Places to visit

**Great North Museum:**
**Hancock Barras Bridge, Newcastle**
**upon Tyne, NE2 4PT, UK**
Investigate how animals survive in
extreme environments in an interactive
Living Planet display.
**www.twmuseums.org.uk/great-north-museum.html**

**Natural History Museum**
**Cromwell Road, London, SW7 5BD, UK**
Explore adaptable animals, massive beasts,
mini-beasts, and life in disguise, both
online and at the museum.
**www.nhm.ac.uk/kids-only/**

**National Museum of Scotland**
**Chambers Street, Edinburgh, EH1 1JF, UK**
The Animal World and Survival galleries
explain why the ability of an animal to
adapt to its environment is the key to its
survival.
**www.nms.ac.uk**

**Oxford Museum of Natural History**
**Parks Road, Oxford, OX1 3PW, UK**
Millions of insects, a bee hive in the
building and touchable dinosaur eggs
**www.oum.ox.ac.uk**
The Pitt Rivers Museum next door also has
an amazing collection.

**Australian Museum**
**6 College Street, Sydney, NSW 2010, Australia**
Find out about dangerous animals of
Australia, spiders, bats, snakes and worms
**http://australianmuseum.net.au/animals**

**American Museum of Natural History**
**Central Park West at 79th Street**
**New York, NY 10024-5192, U.S.A.**
Biodiversity and Environmental halls and
special exhibitions, such as Mysteries
of the Unseen World, which includes
microscopic life, such as fleas.
**www.amnh.org**

**Defenders of Wildlife**
**1130 17th Street NW, Washington, DC 20036, U.S.A.**
Conservation charity that produces online
animal fact sheets, about grizzly bears,
bald eagles, wolverines, bats, wolves, and
more.
**www.defenders.org**

**Monterey Bay Aquarium**
**886 Cannery Row, Monterey, CA, 93940, U.S.A.**
Experience a variety of awesome
underwater creatures, including sharks
and octopuses.
**www.montereybayaquarium.org**

**National Geographic**
Check out the animals and kids pages
and find out how to be a dung beetle or
investigate dog breeds.
**www.nationalgeographic.com/animals**
**http://kids.nationalgeographic.com/kids**

**San Diego Zoo**
**2920 Zoo Drive, San Diego, CA 92101,USA**
Fascinating facts about poison arrow frogs,
anacondas, spiders, scorpions, and more.
**http://zoo.sandiegozoo.org**
**http://kids.sandiegozoo.org**

# Index